Borderline Personality Disorder Survival Guide

Perfect Steps To Managing negative emotions

By

George Gilbert

Copyright

Table of Contents

Conclusion

Introduction

Thank you for visiting the "Borderline Personality Disorder Survival Guide." It's likely that you or a loved one is dealing with borderline personality disorder (BPD) if you're reading this.

The extreme emotional upheaval, the wild mood swings, the difficulties in establishing and maintaining relationships, and the frequently debilitating sensation of emptiness and identity disturbance that can go along with this complicated mental health issue may be causing you pain.

Let us start by reassuring you that you are not alone. The daily hardships brought on by BPD are experienced by millions of people worldwide, and while the path may be difficult, it is not insurmountable. This book is your ally on the road to comprehending, surviving, and eventually thriving despite BPD.

Both persons who have it and those who try to help them may find borderline personality disorder to be a mysterious and baffling disease. It is characterized by a special set of difficulties that might make people feel alone and misunderstood. But it's important to understand that having BPD doesn't make you who you are, and your life doesn't have to revolve around it.

We shall go out on a path of self-discovery, self-empowerment, and resilience-building in this extensive manual. We will go into the fundamentals of BPD, looking at its signs, potential causes, and diagnostic techniques.

More significantly, we will give you the skills and resources you need to navigate the frequently turbulent waters of life with BPD, control the emotional rollercoaster, forge stronger relationships, and so on.

Insights from the most recent psychological and psychiatric research, as well as the knowledge and experiences of people who have battled and overcome BPD, can all be found inside the pages of this book. We'll talk about therapeutic strategies, self-care techniques, and the value of getting professional assistance when you need it.

Our intention is to give you a road map for your own journey of recovery and development. This guide is designed to provide direction, hope, and a sense of community, whether you have recently been diagnosed with BPD, have lived with it for years, or are a friend or family member trying to understand and assist someone with BPD.

Always keep in mind that healing is not a straight line and that setbacks are a normal part of the process. However, you can not only survive but also thrive while living with borderline personality disorder if you have the correct information, resources, and coping mechanisms. We are thrilled to be your mentors as your trip begins right here.

Chapter One:
Understanding Borderline Personality Disorder

In the opening section of the "Borderline Personality Disorder Survival Guide," we set out on a critical understanding trip. Borderline personality disorder (BPD) can frequently seem like an elusive foe, confusing and frustrating sufferers and those close to them.

This chapter tries to clarify the nature of BPD, elucidate its complexities, and give you a strong foundation for the struggles and victories that lie ahead.

We'll begin by defining borderline personality disorder, going over some of its typical signs and behaviors, and digging into its possible causes and risk factors.

The first step to comprehending your own experiences or those of someone you care about is to understand BPD from a clinical standpoint.

We'll also go over the diagnosis and assessment procedure, which will aid you in navigating the occasionally difficult path to a precise diagnosis. A critical step on the road to recovery is acknowledging and admitting the presence of BPD, and we'll help you get through it.

You will have a better knowledge of the monster known as Borderline Personality Disorder by the end of this chapter.

With this information at your disposal, you will be better equipped to handle the difficulties that lie ahead and set out on a path of self-discovery and healing. Let's go in and examine the BPD's roots together.

1.1 Borderline Personality Disorder

What Is Borderline Personality Disorder?

BPD, or borderline personality disorder, is a mental health illness that has a significant impact on a person's thoughts, feelings, and behavior. It's a disorder that can have a big effect on a lot of different things in life such as relationships, self-identity, controlling one's emotions, and general wellbeing.

Patients with this condition frequently experience powerful, quickly changing emotions, which makes it difficult for them to establish stable relationships and a constant sense of self. As a result of this inner turmoil, people may engage in impulsive behaviors like self-harm or drug usage in an effort to cope with their overwhelming feelings.

The fear of abandonment, which can show as a frantic need for connection and, paradoxically, a propensity to push people away, is a defining characteristic of BPD. When people perceive a threat to their relationships, this worry—which frequently arises from a deep-seated fear of rejection or being left alone—can set off dramatic emotions.

In addition, people suffering this illness may experience issues with their sense of self, their sense of self-worth, and feelings of emptiness or boredom. These problems may prolong their suffering and add to their sense of uncertainty.

Recognizing a pattern of these symptoms and behaviors that are pervasive, durable, and outside the norm of ordinary personality functioning is necessary to comprehend the diagnostic criteria for BPD. It's critical to remember that this condition is a medical disorder and not merely a collection of character qualities.

A trained mental health practitioner must evaluate a patient's symptoms and experiences in order to diagnose effectively.
You will have a better understanding of what it means to live with BPD when we discuss these symptoms and behaviors in more detail as we move further into this chapter. This knowledge is the first step in creating practical plans for dealing with borderline personality disorder and eventually prospering.

1.2 Common Signs and Symptoms

A complicated and multidimensional syndrome, borderline personality disorder is characterized by a wide range of symptoms and behaviors. Although the severity and presentation of these symptoms can vary from person to person, they all contribute to the difficulties that BPD sufferers must overcome.

We shall examine some of the disorder's most prevalent and distinguishing symptoms and behaviors in this section:

Intense mood swings: BPD sufferers frequently experience abrupt, significant changes in their emotional condition. They might experience bursts of elation and enthusiasm followed by sudden pangs of melancholy, rage, or anxiety. These mood swings can be challenging to predict and regulate because they might be brought on by seemingly insignificant occurrences.

Fear of Abandonment: A key component of BPD is the fear of abandonment or rejection. When it comes to maintaining relationships, patients may go to tremendous measures, even if it means participating in unhealthy or self-destructive activities, to prevent actual or imagined abandonment.

Impulsive Behavior: People with BPD frequently exhibit impulsivity. Driving recklessly, abusing drugs, bingeing, or injuring oneself are just a few ways this might show up in behavior. These spontaneous behaviors are frequently used as a coping mechanism for strong emotions or as a method to feel in control.

Unstable Relationships: People with BPD may find it difficult to maintain stable, satisfying relationships. Their conflicting idealizations of others can result from their strong emotions and fear of desertion. Relationships may be strained, and frequent arguments may result from this cycle.

Identity Disturbance: Many BPD sufferers have chronic and erratic self-perception. Feelings of emptiness and confusion may result from someone struggling to comprehend their own values, beliefs, and ambitions.

Chronic Emptiness: People with BPD frequently report having a constant feeling of emptiness. They may experience a tremendous void inside of themselves, which prompts them to look for external approval or stimulation to fill this void.

Suicidal Thoughts and Self-Harm: Some people with BPD use self-harming techniques to deal with their emotional anguish. In this population, suicide attempts and ideas are more common. It's critical to take these indications seriously and to get care right away if they appear.

Although these symptoms are typical of BPD, it's crucial to remember that not everyone who has the disease will experience them all, and their severity can vary greatly. Additionally, people with the condition frequently possess distinctive abilities and talents that can be used to advance their recovery process.

We will go into greater detail about the potential causes and risk factors of this disorder, as well as the procedure for diagnosis and assessment, in the following sections of this chapter to give you a thorough grasp of this difficult but treatable disorder.

1.3 Causes and Risk factors

Although the causes of Borderline Personality Disorder are complicated and not entirely understood, scientists have found a number of genetic, environmental, and neurological elements that may play a role in the condition's emergence. It's vital to understand that no one component alone can explain how BPD develops; rather, a mixture of these elements are likely to have an impact on it. Here, we'll examine some of the crucial factors that researchers think contribute to it's emergence.

Evidence exists to support the possibility that the illness has a hereditary component. According to studies, those who have a family history of BPD or other mood disorders may be more likely to have the disorder themselves. However, additional elements must also be present as genetics alone cannot predict the onset of BPD.

Neurobiological Factors: Neuroimaging studies have shown that people with BPD have different brains than people without the condition. These variations could be attributed to issues with emotion control and social cue processing. Particularly, in patients with BPD, the brain regions in charge of impulse control and emotional regulation may be less active or less linked.

Childhood Trauma and Negative Experiences: Many people with BPD have experienced trauma, abuse, or neglect as children. These negative events may have a significant effect on how a person develops emotionally and may also be a factor in the emergence of the symptoms. Not everyone who encounters trauma goes on to develop the illness, and not everyone who has it has gone through trauma.

Environments that Discredit Emotions and Experiences: Growing up in a setting where people disregard one's emotions and experiences can also contribute to the emergence of BPD. This might make people struggle to identify and control their own feelings, which would add to the severe emotional dysregulation seen in BPD.

Biological and Environmental Interaction: It's likely that genetics, brain physiology, and environmental variables interact in a complicated way to cause BPD. Negative events or trauma may lead to the start of BPD in people who have a genetic predisposition that renders them more susceptible to the condition.

In the context of diagnosis and treatment, it can be beneficial to understand these potential causes and risk factors. It's vital to keep in mind that while these factors may raise the possibility of getting this disorder, they do not necessarily guarantee the illness. Contrarily, some people without established risk factors may nevertheless acquire BPD. Many people with risk factors do not develop BPD.

We will explore the diagnostic and assessment process in the section that follows in order to guide you through the critical steps necessary to recognize and comprehend borderline personality disorder.

Chapter 2:
Navigating the Emotional Rollercoaster

One of the most vital side of human experience is feelings. They influence how we think, how we behave, and how we interact with others. Emotions frequently take center stage for those with Borderline Personality Disorder (BPD), and the rollercoaster of emotions can be both thrilling and overpowering.

In this chapter, we set out on a quest to comprehend, control, and ultimately flourish amongst this emotional storm.

BPD is frequently characterized by intense, frequently changing emotions that might be brought on by regular occurrences, other people, or even one's own thoughts. When people experience these emotional highs and lows, it can seem like a never-ending roller coaster, and they find it difficult to reestablish stability and control in their life.

This chapter's objective is to give you useful advice and ideas for controlling these strong emotions. We'll go over how to control your emotions, how to recognize and deal with mood swings, and how to recognize and control the triggers that might cause emotional outbursts.

It is not necessary to deny or suppress feelings in order to navigate the BPD emotional rollercoaster. Instead, it's about taking control of your emotional world, learning to navigate the ebbs and flows, and discovering a feeling of equilibrium that enables you to lead a happy life.

Therefore, buckle up emotionally and get ready to learn how to ride the emotional wave that comes with having borderline personality disorder.

2.1 Controlling Strong Emotions

Living with borderline personality disorder frequently entails coping with high emotions that can also shift quickly. These feelings might consume you completely, making it challenging to concentrate on daily activities or maintain good relationships. However, it is possible to properly regulate these strong emotions with the right techniques. We'll look at methods and resources in this part to help you master your emotional experiences.

Techniques for staying grounded and practicing mindfulness can be quite beneficial for those with BPD. These methods encourage you to remain in the present while objectively observing your thoughts and feelings. When emotions become overwhelming, grounding exercises like the 5-4-3-2-1 approach can also assist in bringing you back to the present moment.

Emotional Awareness: A key component of managing your emotions is becoming more aware of them. Start by mastering precise emotion recognition and labeling. You can more effectively control your emotions if you have self-awareness, which can help you comprehend how and why you're feeling what you're feeling.

Dialectical Behavior Therapy (DBT) is a well-known and scientifically supported therapy strategy for BPD. Enhancing mindfulness, distress tolerance, interpersonal effectiveness, and emotional regulation abilities are its main goals. It can be quite advantageous to learn these abilities in a structured environment.

Emotional regulation strategies are provided by DBT and other therapy modalities for dealing with strong emotions. These may include techniques like "opposite action" (behaving in a way that is incongruent with the emotion), "ABC PLEASE" (an abbreviation for distress tolerance), and "checking the situation."and facts" (evaluating how accurate your emotional reactions are).

Self-Reflection and Journaling: Keeping a journal to record your thoughts and feelings can be a helpful tool. You can track your improvement in managing your emotions by using this technique to help you spot patterns in your emotional experiences.

Seeking Support: If you're experiencing strong emotions, don't be afraid to ask for help. During trying times, trusted friends, family members, or support groups can provide compassion and consolation. Additionally, professional counseling can give you personalized emotional management techniques.

Healthy lifestyle practices: Your emotional condition can be greatly influenced by your physical health. Setting regular exercise, a healthy diet, and sufficient sleep as top priorities will help you manage your emotions and increase your emotional toughness in general.
Keep in mind that controlling strong emotions requires continual effort, and it's acceptable to seek help.

You may better manage your emotions and ride the emotional rollercoaster by implementing these techniques into your daily life and engaging with a mental health expert. In the sections that follow, we'll go into more detail on managing mood swings and identifying your triggers.

2.2 Managing Mood Swings

Living with Borderline Personality Disorder (BPD) involves dealing with mood fluctuations frequently and can be difficult. Although these abrupt changes in emotional states might be draining and confusing, there are coping mechanisms you can use.

This section will examine methods and strategies for controlling and comprehending mood swings:

Maintaining a mood journal might help you identify the patterns and factors that lead to your mood changes. Keep track of the circumstances, happenings, or ideas that match up with changes in your feelings. This log may offer insightful information about your emotional triggers over time.

Creating a Crisis Plan: When experiencing severe mood swings, having a crisis plan in place can be quite beneficial. This strategy could contain a contact list, coping techniques to attempt, and a reminder of the value of getting professional assistance when necessary.

Distraction tactics can offer momentary comfort when you're feeling overpowered by strong emotions. Reading, solving puzzles, or engaging in creative hobbies can all serve as effective distractions from painful thoughts and emotions.

Emotional Regulation Skills: As was already noted, DBT-style techniques, such as dialectical behavior therapy (DBT), teach clients how to regulate their emotions. These abilities show you how to control your emotional responses and seize the initiative when your mood starts to change.

Practices for mindfulness and grounding can keep you anchored in the present and help you control your emotions by preventing them from spiraling out of control. These methods are especially helpful when you start to feel a mood change coming on.

Self-Care Rituals: Creating a self-care regimen can provide your everyday life stability and regularity. Give self-care practices like relaxation techniques, meditation, or time spent in nature that support emotional well-being first priority.

Medication: In certain circumstances, taking medication that has been prescribed by a mental health expert may help stabilize mood swings. The emotional instability linked to BPD can be effectively managed with drugs like mood stabilizers or certain antidepressants.

Supportive Relationships: For assistance through mood fluctuations, rely on close friends and family. Tell them what you can do to help, or just be there to listen without passing judgment. Social support is an effective tool for managing BPD.

While these coping mechanisms can be helpful, it's crucial to keep in mind that mood fluctuations might still occur. BPD is a complicated illness, and treating its symptoms requires constant effort. Be patient with yourself and keep seeking out expert advice to create individualized plans that will work the best for you.

Identifying and comprehending triggers, which can be crucial in the onset of mood swings and emotional turbulence, will be the focus of the next section.

2.3 Recognizing Triggers

Events, circumstances, or thoughts known as triggers cause extreme emotional reactivity or mood swings in people with borderline personality disorder (BPD). Finding these triggers is an essential first step in controlling your emotional reactions and improving your emotional wellbeing. This section will examine techniques for identifying and comprehending your particular triggers:

Self-Reflection: Start by considering your previous emotional outbursts and mood swings. Take into account the circumstances of these encounters. Were there particular events, persons, or ideas that always came before these emotional changes?

Journaling: Keeping a thorough record of your thoughts, feelings, and everyday experiences can be a very helpful tool for figuring out triggers. Write down your thoughts, feelings, and actions prior to any substantial mood swings you become aware of.

Therapy and expert assistance can help you more effectively identify triggers, especially those who have experience treating BPD. You can examine your emotional reactions in therapy sessions and identify typical triggers with your therapist.

Identifying Patterns: As time passes, you might start to recognize patterns in your triggers. You can discover, for instance, that particular criticism, rejection, or social circumstances consistently cause strong emotional reactions. Finding these patterns might be a crucial step in staying away from

Emotional Awareness: As we covered in the last section, increasing your emotional awareness can also help you spot triggers. You'll be better able to spot when your emotions start to change unpredictably as you become more aware of them.

Communication with Others: Honest, open dialogue with dependable friends, family members, or partners might yield insightful information. They may pick up on patterns or triggers that you miss, and they can help you avoid or manage these triggers.

Avoidance When Required: In some circumstances, it may be wise to steer clear of well-known triggers whenever feasible. For instance, if a specific social circumstance routinely causes emotional pain, you might want to restrict your exposure to it or come up with coping mechanisms for when you must face it.

After you've determined your triggers, having a variety of coping techniques at your disposal is crucial. These approaches, including deep breathing, mindfulness, or diversionary tactics, can assist you in controlling the emotional reactions brought on by particular circumstances or ideas.

Keep in mind that every person with BPD has a different set of triggers that need to be identified and managed. It's crucial to concentrate on your own experiences and desires because what triggers one person could not trigger another. You may significantly improve your emotional stability and well-being by understanding your triggers and creating techniques to deal with them.

Chapter Three:
Building Healthy Relationship

Healthy and fulfilling relationships are vital to our well-being, but for individuals with Borderline Personality Disorder (BPD), navigating the complexities of human connections can be particularly challenging. BPD often manifests in patterns of idealizing and devaluing others, intense fears of abandonment, and frequent interpersonal conflicts. In this chapter, we will embark on a journey to explore the intricacies of forming and maintaining healthy relationships while living with BPD.

Building healthy relationships is not just about managing the symptoms of BPD but also about fostering connections that support your well-being and personal growth. Whether you're seeking to improve existing relationships or forge new ones, this chapter will provide you with insights, strategies, and skills to create and maintain meaningful connections.

The chapter will cover a variety of relationship-building topics, such as clear communication, setting boundaries, handling disagreements, and creating supportive relationships. You'll have a toolkit of strategies and a better knowledge of how to negotiate the tricky terrain of relationships while dealing with borderline personality disorder at the end of this chapter.

3.1 Relationship difficulties

Relationship building and maintenance can be particularly difficult for those who have borderline personality disorder (BPD). These difficulties frequently result from the qualities and behaviors that characterize the disease. We will look at a few of the typical relationship issues that people with BPD may have in this section:

Idealization and Devaluation: The propensity to idealize people at one point but denigrate them at another is a distinguishing trait of BPD. Relationships can become strained as a result of this black-and-white thinking because people with BPD find it difficult to see both sides of an issue.

Fear of Abandonment: For those with BPD, the fear of abandonment is a major and continuous worry. This anxiety can result in excessive clinginess, valiant attempts to prevent abandonment, or the preemptive rejection of others in an effort to safeguard oneself against perceived abandonment.

When it comes to relationships, people with BPD often struggle with emotionally intense reactions. Arguments and confrontations can result from little differences or perceived slights because they can cause strong emotional responses.

Boundary Issues: People with BPD may find it difficult to establish and enforce limits. They might struggle to respect others' boundaries or struggle to set their own, which can result in disagreements and miscommunication.

Impulsivity: Impulsive actions, such as carelessly squandering money or making snap judgments, can have a detrimental effect on relationships. These behaviors may put financial stability at risk and cause friction with loved ones or romantic partners.

Dissociation: Dissociative episodes, in which people experience a sense of disconnection from reality or from themselves, can obstruct clear communication and emotional ties in relationships.

Identity Disturbance: Having a shaky sense of who you are might make it difficult to build solid, long-lasting connections. Without a firm grasp of oneself, it is difficult to communicate and connect with others in a genuine way.

Even though these difficulties are frequent in relationships including BPD, it's important to understand that they are not insurmountable difficulties. The correct tactics, insight, and self-awareness can help people with BPD form relationships that are healthier and more meaningful.

We will examine useful methods and abilities for overcoming these difficulties in the areas that follow in this chapter, including effective communication, establishing boundaries, and preserving supportive relationships. You can learn and hone the skill of creating and maintaining healthy relationships, and this chapter will serve as your manual for doing so.

3.2 Skills in Effective Communication

Healthy relationships are built on effective communication, which is also essential for overcoming the special difficulties that people with Borderline Personality Disorder (BPD) frequently experience. The quality of your relationships can be greatly enhanced by learning how to communicate your thoughts and feelings effectively, listen intently, and settle problems in a constructive manner. In this section, we'll look at a variety of communication techniques that can make relationship management easier for you.

Effective communication can be improved through mindfulness, which encourages present-moment awareness and nonjudgmental listening. Practice listening intently to the other person during conversations and refraining from making snap decisions or assumptions.

Giving someone your complete attention and demonstrating empathy is part of active listening. Make an attempt to comprehend their viewpoint, get more information from them, and respect their emotions. This method encourages a feeling of being heard and comprehended.

I-Statements: Try utilizing "I" statements to convey your thoughts and feelings rather than accusing "you" comments. Say "I feel hurt when..." instead of "You always make me feel..." as an example.

Empathy: Empathy entails understanding the feelings and experiences of the other person by placing oneself in their position. Empathy expression encourages emotional intimacy and connection in relationships.

In order to validate someone's feelings, you must first acknowledge their emotions and demonstrate your understanding of their motivations, even if you don't necessarily share them. Validation is useful to reduce conflict intensity and enhance communication.

Avoiding Blame and Accusations: Conflicts can be swiftly exacerbated by blaming and accusing others. Instead, concentrate on communicating your wants and feelings without blaming others. Conversations may become more fruitful as a result of this change in communication.

Conflict Resolution Skills: In any relationship, being able to handle problems in a constructive manner is crucial. Compromise, "I-statements," and active listening are techniques that can be used to settle disputes amicably.

Setting Boundaries: Establishing and conveying your own boundaries clearly is essential for happy relationships. Be adamant about your requirements and limitations, and inspire others to follow suit. For respect and trust to be intact, boundaries must be respected.

Emotional Regulation: Use emotional regulation strategies, including deep breathing or mindfulness, before having a potentially challenging talk will help you maintain calm and composure ask the talk proceed.

Seeking Expert Assistance: Couples or family therapy with a qualified mental health practitioner may occasionally be helpful in enhancing communication and addressing relationship difficulties caused by BPD.

These interpersonal skills can be helpful for anybody trying to improve their interpersonal interactions, not only those with BPD, in establishing and sustaining healthy relationships. It's important to keep in mind that effective communication is a talent that can be cultivated and improved through time, so there is never a bad time to start.

3.3 Creating Limits

Setting and upholding boundaries is essential to creating and sustaining good relationships, particularly for those who suffer from Borderline Personality Disorder (BPD). Boundaries help both parties feel respected and at ease by outlining the parameters and expectations of a partnership. We will discuss the significance of setting boundaries in this part, as well as provide advice on how to do so successfully:

Boundaries should be understood as guidelines that specify how you want to be treated and how you will treat others rather than as barriers that separate you from others. They specify what conduct is appropriate and inappropriate in a partnership.

Self-Awareness: Begin by developing a profound grasp of your own requirements, ideals, and constraints. A crucial component of communication is being aware of oneself and your boundaries.

Clear and honest communication are essential for healthy boundaries. With individuals who are close to you, talk about your limits and why they are necessary for both your wellbeing and the wellbeing of the relationship.

Consistency: When it comes to limits, consistency is essential. Consistently uphold your limits to foster a sense of dependability and trust in your interactions.

Respecting Others' Boundaries: Be careful of respecting others' boundaries, just as you would expect others to do for you. This reciprocity is essential for developing respect and trust among people. While boundaries are necessary, they shouldn't be impermeable or hard. Be prepared to adapt your boundaries as your circumstances or you as a person change.

Saying "No" When It's Necessary: Creating boundaries frequently entails refusing requests when doing so will endanger your health. A crucial skill is the ability to politely and assertively refuse requests or demands.

Knowing When Someone Has Crossed Your Boundaries: Be diligent in knowing when someone has crossed your boundaries. It's critical to address the situation as soon as you feel uncomfortable or violated in an authoritative manner..

Getting Support: If you have trouble establishing and upholding boundaries, think about getting help from a therapist or counselor. These experts help in providing instructions that can suit your personal preference.

Make self-care a priority to preserve your mental and physical wellbeing. You are more able to establish and uphold limits when you are taking care of yourself. Keep in mind that establishing and successfully maintaining boundaries may require some time as it is a continuous process.

Healthy boundaries can help you negotiate the difficulties that BPD frequently brings along by fostering healthier, more respectful relationships. The portions of this chapter that follow will go through methods for handling disagreements and creating supportive relationships, which will help you develop your relationship-building abilities even more.

Chapter 4:

Coping with Self-Destructive Behaviors in BPD

The self-destructive behaviors that borderline personality disorder (BPD) patients frequently engage in are stressful and difficult to deal with. These behaviors can appear in a variety of ways, such as self-harm, impulsive conduct, drug use, and careless decision-making. We will explore the complexities of self-destructive habits in this chapter, including their underlying causes, coping mechanisms, and when to seek professional assistance.

Understanding that self-destructive behaviors are frequently motivated by severe emotional pain and the need to deal with overpowering feelings, it is crucial to approach this chapter with empathy and understanding. Our objective is to give you knowledge, resources, and strategies to address and control these habits in a healthier and more beneficial way.

You can significantly enhance your mental well-being and general quality of life while managing with BPD by developing a greater understanding of self-destructive behaviors and picking up helpful coping techniques.

4.1 Impulsivity and Self-Harm

Among the most alarming and unpleasant self-destructive behaviors linked to Borderline Personality Disorder (BPD), self-harm and impulsivity. It's critical to approach these behaviors with care and respect because they can carry serious hazards to one's physical and emotional health. We will examine self-harm and impulsivity in further detail in this part, including their potential causes, warning signals, and coping mechanisms:

Self-Harm: Self-harm is the deliberate infliction of physical harm on oneself as a coping mechanism for emotional suffering, to manage intense emotions, or to reclaim control.

Impulsivity: In the context of BPD, impulsivity refers to acting on strong emotions without taking into account the possible repercussions. Impulsive behaviors might include dangerous sexual conduct, binge eating, driving while intoxicated, and reckless spending.

4.2 Knowing the Root Causes

Impulsivity and self-harm are frequent attempts to dull or lessen strong emotions or emotional anguish. They can provide a misleading sensation of relief or a brief escape from emotional turbulence. The first step in effectively managing self-destructive behaviors is to recognize the emotional and psychological factors that cause them.

Warning Symbols: Self-harm and impulsivity have warning indicators, and both people with BPD and their support systems must be aware of these signs. Unexpected scrapes or bruises, a habit of rash decisions, or a change in mood are just a few examples of warning signals of a history of toxic tendency. It's very important to see these signs as a special case without judging it's appropriateness.

4.3 Coping Techniques

Coping with strong feelings is simply making better options available to replace your irrational actions. Below are some of the strategies that can help you overcome such feelings.

Distraction Strategies Focus-demanding pursuits like deep breathing techniques, music, exercise, or art might help you turn your attention away from dangerous urges.

Prioritize self-care activities like mindfulness, meditation, and relaxation techniques that support emotional well-being.

Emotional Regulation Techniques: Techniques acquired through therapies like Dialectical Behavior Therapy (DBT) can be quite successful in controlling impulsivity. These abilities show you how to control your emotional outbursts and make more deliberate choices.

Seeking Professional treatment: It's critical to seek professional treatment if self-harm and impulsivity are severe or persistent. Specialized therapies and interventions can be provided by mental health specialists to address these issues. these actions.
Keep in mind that eliminating self-destructive behaviors requires effort and may result in setbacks.

Be kind to yourself and ask for help from dependable people and experts. We will examine alternatives to self-harm, the significance of getting professional assistance, and self-help techniques for controlling destructive inclinations in the sections of this chapter that follow.

4.4 Options Rather Than Self-Harm

Since self-destructive habits can be harmful, it's important to look into healthy alternatives that can provide relief without endangering physical health or putting an individual's emotional wellbeing at risk. In this section, we'll talk about different coping mechanisms that people with borderline personality disorder (BPD) can employ when they feel strong emotions or the urge to act out.

Grounding and mindfulness:
Practicing mindfulness can help you focus on the present moment and manage rising emotions without resorting to self-harm. Exercises for establishing a solid foundation, like the 5-4-3-2-1 approach, can also establish a sense of stability when you're have emotional crisis.

Expressive Arts: Engaging in creative activities like writing, playing an instrument, or sketching can be a safe and effective method to express your emotions and direct them toward a creative project.

Exercise: Taking part in physical activities like yoga, dance, or running might help you let go of tension and lessen mental suffering. Endorphins, which are believed to naturally elevate mood, are known to be released after exercise.

Self-Soothing Methods: Amass a collection of calming and reassuring self-soothing methods. To do this, you might take a warm bath, drink herbal tea, practice deep breathing, or use calming scents like lavender or chamomile.

Welfare: Talk to your loved ones or support group where the tendencies to contain your thoughts to harm yourself goes out of control. Establishing relationships with people who are sensitive to your difficulties will be helpful in redirecting your attention away from self-harm.

Create a list of emergency contacts that you can call upon in case of an emergency. These contacts may be a crisis hotline, therapist, or counselor.

Create a crisis plan that describes what to do when the impulse to self-destruct becomes strong. This plan may include suggestions, contact information, and tools for getting help right away.

Consider receiving therapy that focuses on developing emotional regulation skills and finding better ways to deal with strong emotions, such as dialectical behavior therapy (DBT).

Writing in a journal can aid in the understanding and processing of your ideas and feelings. It can provide a secure platform for personal expression.

Progress tracking: Honor your accomplishments in avoiding impulsive actions and self-harm. Keep track of the instances you were able to deal without hurting yourself, and use those successes as inspiration to keep looking for healthier solutions.

It's crucial to keep in mind that selecting the best alternate coping mechanisms could need some trial and error. It's worthy to note that one person's solution might not be suitable for another. So being kind to yourself and willing to try out numerous strategies will be a great idea. This should continue until you find one that enables you to control your irrational thoughts without putting yourself in harm's way. Seeking Help From Experts

Dealing with self-destructive habits frequently calls for professional treatment and advice, especially when they are linked to Borderline Personality Disorder (BPD). A critical first step in discovering the underlying reasons of these behaviors and creating efficient management and overcoming techniques is to seek assistance from mental health professionals.

This section will discuss the value of seeking professional assistance as well as the different kinds of therapy that may be helpful:

The function of mental health specialists: Therapists, counselors, and psychiatrists are among the mental health specialists qualified to identify and address self-destructive BPD behaviors.

You can explore the underlying causes of your behavior and create healthy coping skills in their secure and nonjudgmental environment.

Individual Therapy: When it comes to resolving self-destructive behaviors, one-on-one therapy, such as Dialectical Behavior Therapy (DBT) or Cognitive-Behavioral Therapy (CBT), can be quite successful. Your therapist can help you identify triggers, create coping mechanisms, and improve your ability to control your emotions.

Group Therapy: Group therapy sessions provide you the chance to connect with people going through similar struggles. Peer learning and experience sharing can help people feel supported and understood.

Medication: In some situations, taking medication that has been recommended to you by a psychiatrist may help you control self-destructive habits. The underlying mental problems or impulsivity that cause these behaviors can be treated with medication.

Crisis Intervention: When you get a deep feeling of hurting yourself, do hesitate to seek help. Emergency medical services, crisis hotlines, and crisis centers are handy to supply urgent help.

Long-Term Treatment: It is frequently necessary to receive continuing care and support in order to stop self-destructive habits. A rehabilitation road map can be created in conjunction with mental health specialists as part of a treatment strategy.

Family therapy or including loved ones in your treatment can be beneficial. It can promote understanding, enhance family interactions, and assist in educating them regarding BPD and self-destructive behaviors.

Commitment to your treatment plan and consistency in attendance at therapy sessions are crucial. The process of recovering from self-destructive behaviors is gradual, and it could take some time before you start to notice any real progress.

Self-advocacy: Be an active participant in your care by being transparent with the mental health experts who are treating you. Share your achievements, obstacles, and any treatment-related worries.

Keep in mind that asking for help from a professional is a sign of strength and endurance. To handle your strong emotions probably, you can consult mental health experts. With the correct assistance, you may strive toward living a healthier and more happy life. You don't have to deal with these difficulties alone.

Chapter Five:
Overcoming Loneliness and Isolation

Individuals with Borderline Personality Disorder (BPD) may have intense and unpleasant experiences with isolation and loneliness. BPD's turbulent nature, coupled with issues controlling emotions and relationships, frequently causes people to feel alone and cut off from others.

This chapter will examine how loneliness affects mental and emotional health and provide methods for overcoming these isolating emotions. Developing a sense of self-worth and self-acceptance is just as important for overcoming loneliness and isolation as forging new relationships with people outside of oneself.

The objective is to arm you with knowledge, resources, and doable actions that will enable you to rebuild your relationships with others and, more significantly, with yourself. This chapter will give you a better knowledge of how to manoeuver and overcome the isolating part of suffering Borderline personality Disorder.

5.1 Understanding isolation and loneliness

Understanding what loneliness and isolation are and how they relate to borderline personality disorder (BPD) is crucial before we can address and overcome these feelings. We will examine the subtle nuances of isolation and loneliness in this section, especially as they relate to BPD:

Loneliness: The subjective experience of being cut off from others or lacking deep social relationships is known as loneliness. Even when you are physically surrounded by people, it can still happen. A feeling of emptiness, solitude, and a desire for meaningful interactions are frequently present companions to loneliness.

On the other hand, isolation describes a situation in which one is physically or socially cut off from others. Self-imposed seclusion or a lack of opportunity for relationship. Isolation can arouse the sense loneliness and makes one want think of being rejected.

BPD and loneliness: People with BPD frequently suffer loneliness and isolation for a variety of reasons, including:

Intense Emotional States: People with BPD frequently experience a rollercoaster of emotions, which can cause them to withdraw from social situations because they worry about upsetting other people.

Fear of Abandonment: One of the main characteristics of BPD is the fear of abandonment, which can cause a person to withdraw from relationships in advance of what they see as rejection.

Interpersonal Conflicts: People with BPD may avoid social situations in an effort to avoid interpersonal conflicts, which can lead to a vicious cycle of isolation.

Negative Self-Image: People with a negative self-image, another prevalent feature of BPD, may isolate themselves because they feel unworthy of friendships.

Stigma and Misunderstanding: BPD is stigmatized and misunderstood, which makes it difficult to get help and understanding from others and exacerbates feelings of isolation.

The first step in properly treating these issues is to grasp the nuances of loneliness and isolation in the context of BPD. The tactics for re-connecting with people, creating deep connections, and fostering a feeling of belonging and self-acceptance will be covered in the parts that follow in this chapter.

5.2 Techniques for Reconnecting

With Borderline Personality Disorder (BPD) in particular, overcoming loneliness and isolation calls for intentional efforts and a dedication to creating and fostering connections. In this part, we'll look into useful techniques that can assist you in making new connections and building a network of people who understand and support your journey:

Self-Acceptance: Begin by working on your own self-acceptance. Recognize that despite BPD's problems, you are deserving of love and connection. Celebrate your accomplishments and your success in disorder management.

Reach Out to Reliable People: List a few reliable, understanding, and sympathetic friends or family members. Tell them what's on your mind and how you feel, and let them know how they can help. Making the initial contact might occasionally result in a closer relationship.

Join Support Groups: Take into account joining a support group that is especially for people with BPD. These groups offer a secure setting for connecting with people who have gone through similar things, providing both empathy and useful guidance.

Treatment: Addressing the loneliness and isolation brought on by BPD can be accomplished through individual treatment. You may discover the underlying reasons of these emotions and create plans to create healthy relationships with the aid of a competent therapist.

Develop Your Social Skills: If you find it difficult to engage with people owing to your isolation, you might want to explore developing your social skills. Begin with easy actions like striking up casual conversations or going to social gatherings with a reliable buddy.

Volunteer or Join Activities: Volunteering or joining activities that interest you may be great ways to meet others who share your interests and form connections with them.

Online Communities: Although face-to-face interactions are crucial, online communities and forums may foster a feeling of community and comprehension. Be careful how you balance online and offline relationships.

Limits: Keep in mind how crucial it is to establish and uphold limits when you re-connect with individuals. Mutual respect and an appreciation of each other's limitations are the foundation of healthy partnerships.

Continue honing your emotional control and mindfulness techniques to deal with any strong emotions that may surface during social encounters. You can stay grounded and avoid misunderstandings with the aid of these abilities.

Acknowledge and appreciate your connections-building efforts, no matter how modest it may be. Recognize the bravery required to overcome isolation and loneliness.

It's important to keep in mind that conquering loneliness and isolation is a process that may include setbacks. Be kind to yourself and understand that, even when coping with BPD, developing deep relationships and a support network is feasible. By making deliberate decisions and asking for help, you can establish a feeling of acceptance and reduce feeling of rejection.

5.3 Creating Meaningful Connections

A key objective in overcoming loneliness and isolation when dealing with Borderline Personality Disorder (BPD) is to develop meaningful relationships. Emotional support, comprehension, and a sense of belonging can all be obtained via meaningful interactions. We will look at methods for establishing and maintaining such interactions in this section:

Accept Vulnerability: Vulnerability is frequently necessary for meaningful interactions. With someone you can trust, give yourself permission to be open and honest about your feelings, opinions, and experiences. Greater knowledge and relationships can result from vulnerability.

Successful Communication: In your relationships, use the successful communication techniques we covered previously in this guide. The effectiveness of your conversations may be improved through active listening, empathy, and the explicit expressing of thoughts and feelings.

Making New Connections: Look for chances to network and broaden your social circle. This can entail going to social gatherings, joining organizations or hobby groups, or being involved in neighborhood activities.

Shared Interests and Hobbies: Developing connections based on interests and pastimes in common can lay a strong basis for communication. Take part in things you are enthusiastic about, and you'll probably come across others who share your interests.

Realistic expectations must be set if you want your relationships to succeed. Conflicts and arguments are a normal aspect of every relationship since nobody is perfect. Your relationships can become stronger if you learn how to overcome these obstacles in a positive way.

Empathy and compassion: Develop empathy and compassion for both yourself and others. Recognize that everyone has challenges, and that developing empathy may result in relationships that are more forgiving and kind.

Quality Over Quantity: The strength of the ties between people is more important than their quantity. Instead than trying to be everything to everyone, concentrate on cultivating a few genuine relationships.

Maintaining appropriate limits in your relationships is important. Boundaries help you preserve your sense of self within a connection and make sure that your demands and boundaries are honored.

Consider obtaining advice from a therapist or counselor if previous relationships have been tough or if you are having trouble forming and maintaining ties. They can support you.

Express your thanks for the connections you have and the assistance you get on a regular basis. Your appreciation for important interactions may be enhanced through gratitude.

The process of creating lasting connections takes time, effort, and self-awareness. You may lessen feelings of loneliness and isolation while developing a sense of belonging and support in your life by putting these methods into practice and being proactive in seeking out and maintaining relationships.

5.4 Building a Self-Worth Foundation

A key component of overcoming loneliness and isolation when dealing with Borderline Personality Disorder (BPD) is developing a strong sense of self-worth. Feelings of worthlessness and self-doubt can be caused by low self-esteem and can make it difficult to build deep relationships.

We'll look at several methods in this part to help you develop and maintain a strong feeling of your own worth:

Practice self-compassion: Be kind and compassionate to oneself as you would a friend going through a difficult time. Self-compassion entails accepting your flaws and, rather than self-criticism, reacting to them with understanding.

Challenge Negative Self-Talk: Always be mindful of your internal dialogue and tackle them as they occur. Replace negative self-talk with thoughtful, empathetic ones. Cognitive-behavioral methods may be helpful here.

List your abilities, assets, and good traits. Recognize and celebrate your strengths. Celebrate all of your accomplishments, no matter how minor they may appear, and often remind yourself of these qualities.

Create Achievable objectives: Create objectives that are in line with your beliefs and interests. A sense of purpose and a boost in self-esteem might come from achieving these goals.

Seek Internal Validation: Rely less on external validation and other people's acceptance. Instead, concentrate on validating yourself by recognising your successes and deciding for yourself that you are worthy regardless of what others may think.

Self-Care: Give self-care routines that advance your mental and physical health top priority. Self-care activities might help you communicate how much you respect yourself.

Spend time with positive people who will encourage and support you. Surround yourself with positivity. Positive influences can help you combat poor self-perceptions.

Self-Reflection and Mindfulness: Practices for mindfulness can help you stay present and judgment-free. Your comprehension of yourself and your needs can be further enhanced via self-reflection.

Create Achievable objectives: Create objectives that are in line with your beliefs and interests. A sense of purpose and a boost in self-esteem might come from achieving these goals.

Seek Internal Validation: Rely less on external validation and other people's acceptance. Instead, concentrate on validating yourself by recognising your successes and deciding for yourself that you are worthy regardless of what others may think.

Self-Care: Give self-care routines that advance your mental and physical health top priority. Self-care activities might help you communicate how much you respect yourself.

Spend time with positive people who will encourage and support you. Surround yourself with positivity. Positive influences can help you combat poor self-perceptions.

Self-Reflection and Mindfulness: Practices for mindfulness can help you stay present and judgment-free. Additionally, self-reflection can help you better grasp who you are and what you need.

Professional Assistance: If self-esteem problems are pervasive or have a big influence on your life, think about getting help from a therapist or counselor. A disciplined and encouraging setting like therapy might be helpful for addressing underlying self-worth problems.

It takes persistence and self-compassion to develop a sense of worth in oneself. You may strengthen the basis for meaningful interactions and lessen the negative effects of loneliness and isolation in your life by putting these methods into practice and focusing on your self-esteem.

Accepting Loneliness as a Positive Option

While eliminating isolation and loneliness is a crucial objective, it's equally critical to understand that solitude, when accepted as a good decision, may be an important aspect of your life. In contrast to loneliness, solitude entails a deliberate choice to spend time with oneself for purposes of introspection, self-care, and personal development. The advantages of embracing isolation and how it may support your efforts to treat borderline personality disorder (BPD) are covered in the following sections:

Self-Reflection: Solitude offers a chance for introspection and self-awareness. It gives you access to a private, contemplative setting where you may examine your ideas, feelings, and morals.

Spending time alone may be a powerful method to decompress and relieve stress. It gives you a respite from the obligations and interpersonal contacts of daily life, enabling you to unwind and regenerate.

Productivity and Creativity: Solitude may encourage both of these traits. It offers a setting that is favorable for in-depth contemplation, problem-solving, and discovering new ideas.

Emotional Regulation: By allowing you the time and space to absorb and control strong emotions, solitude can help with emotional regulation. You can exercise mindfulness and self-soothing methods.

Practicing solitude is a kind of self-care. It enables you to set priorities for your requirements, partake in enjoyable activities, and restore your mental and emotional vitality.

Solitude encourages independence and self-reliance. Learning to appreciate your own company and rely on oneself for enjoyment and comfort can increase your self-esteem.

Reducing Dependence on Others: For people with BPD, it's crucial to lessen their reliance on others for emotional support and affirmation. You can learn to better manage your emotional wellbeing by spending more time alone.

Solitude is a good approach to establish sound limits in your life. It makes it possible for you to strike a balance between social engagements and personal leisure, ensuring that your health always comes first.

Embracing solitude as a decision rather than a result of isolation gives you the power to take charge of your social connections. It changes the narrative such that being alone is now a choice rather than a necessity.

Balance is important for general well-being since it allows for both social interaction and alone time. When you embrace solitude as a good decision, you may benefit from both connection and alone time.

Remember that solitude should not be a strategy for avoiding social encounters or maintaining isolation, but rather a deliberate and informed decision. You may improve your self-awareness, emotional resiliency, and general quality of life while living with BPD by embracing isolation in a healthy and balanced way.

5. Positive Solitude Practices

Making a conscious effort to interact with and take use of your alone time is part of cultivating happy solitude. The following tips can assist you in getting the most out of your solitude:

Set specific objectives for what you expect to accomplish or experience during a period of isolation before beginning. Having a goal for your isolation may make it more meaningful, whether that goal is self-reflection, relaxation, creativity, or personal development.

Make a Space for Solitude: Establish a physical location where you can go to have some alone time. Whether you're reading, writing in a diary, practicing meditation, or just taking a time to yourself, this area should be relaxing, distraction-free, and conducive to your chosen hobbies.

Disconnect from Technology: Being alone is a great way to get away from the continual clamor and interruptions of technology. To completely experience the present moment during your alone time, think about switching off your electronics or putting them away.

Practice awareness: When you're alone, choose activities that encourage awareness. Deep breathing exercises, thoughtful walks in nature, and other mindfulness techniques might help you become more self-aware and better manage your emotions.

Writing in a diary may be a helpful approach to process your thoughts and feelings while you're alone. Write about your insights, experiences, and any difficulties you may be having. Your alone time might feel more complete and clearer if you keep a journal.

Use your alone as a chance to engage in self-care. Spend time doing things that feed your body and mind, including having a long bath, doing something you like, or just relaxing and recharging.

Establish Healthy Boundaries: Make sure others in your life respect your need for privacy. Set limits that safeguard your personal time and space and express the desire for alone time.

Learn to appreciate Your Own Company: Learning to appreciate your own company is frequently necessary to embrace isolation. Consider it an opportunity to get to know yourself better and appreciate your own traits and viewpoints rather than seeing it as being alone.

Practice Gratitude: In your time alone, consider the things in your life for which you are thankful. Your attention might be drawn away from what you might be missing and toward what you do have and value.

Assess Your Development: Check in with yourself sometimes to see how your practice of solitude is helping you. Are you succeeding in your goals? Do you feel more relaxed, self-aware, or creative? If necessary, modify your strategy to maximize your experience.

You may make alone time a useful tool for self-care, self-growth, and personal fulfillment by making a conscious effort to cultivate happy solitude. This supports your efforts to By enabling you to develop a deeper connection with yourself, you may combat loneliness and isolation and improve your capacity to genuinely connect with others.

Chapter Six:
Managing Emotional Intensity

Borderline personality disorder (BPD) is characterized by emotional intensity, which frequently offers particular difficulties for people with this disorder. Rapid mood swings and the extreme highs and lows can have an adverse effect on everyday living, interpersonal connections, and general wellbeing. We'll look at practical methods for controlling emotional intensity in this chapter, giving you the skills you need to traverse these choppy emotional seas with more steadiness and fortitude.

For persons with BPD, comprehending and resolving emotional intensity is crucial since it can cause impulsive conduct, relational issues, and a higher risk of self-destructive behavior. You may obtain a higher feeling of emotional balance and well-being by acquiring understanding of the nature of emotional intensity and learning useful strategies to control it.

6.1 Recognizing Trigger And Pattern

The capacity to recognize the triggers and patterns that contribute to high emotional reactions is one of the key elements in controlling emotional intensity. Patterns are repeating themes or behaviors that enhance these emotions, whereas triggers are circumstances, events, or ideas that cause intense emotional reactions. It's critical to recognize trends and triggers in order to create efficient emotional management techniques.

How to do it is as follows:

- Start by maintaining a diary to document your feelings and experiences. Note the specifics around any strong emotional reactions you see. Include any background information, your thoughts, bodily sensations, and any events that occurred before the emotional outburst.

- Examine your diary entries frequently to look for recurring themes or patterns. Are there particular persons, events, or ideas that constantly cause you to feel highly charged? You may get ready for potential triggers by noticing repeated trends.

- Emotion tracking: As your feelings arise, classify them using a straightforward technique. This might make it simpler for you to identify and handle the most severe and frequent emotional states.

- Request Feedback: You can get insightful feedback on your emotional triggers and patterns from dependable friends, family members, or a therapist. They could see trends that you are unaware of and provide an alternative viewpoint.

- Practice mindfulness and self-awareness to become more aware of your emotional reactions in the present. Being mindful enables you to objectively watch your emotion for greater results.

- To work with a professional in recognizing and resolving emotional triggers and patterns, think about counseling, specifically Dialectical Behavior counseling (DBT) or Cognitive-Behavioral Therapy (CBT). Therapists can offer direction and methods customized to your unique need.

- Take regular breaks for self-reflection to examine the underlying reasons behind your emotional responses. Why do particular circumstances or ideas make you feel such strong emotions? It is possible to gain more self-awareness through this introspection.

- Pay attention to any bodily sensations that are connected to a person's level of emotional intensity. Indicators of heightened emotional states include tight muscles, a quick heartbeat, shallow breathing, and other physical manifestations.

The first step to properly controlling emotional intensity is recognizing your emotional triggers and patterns. When you are aware of what causes your strong emotions, you can take action. As you start to build coping mechanisms, the negative effects these triggers have on your day-to-day activities and interpersonal connections will lessen.

6.2 Emotional Regulations Techniques

For those with Borderline Personality Disorder (BPD), emotional regulation methods are crucial tools for efficiently managing powerful emotions. These methods provide you the power to control your emotional outbursts, lessen suffering, and make better decisions.

We'll look at a variety of techniques in this part to help you control your emotions, including:

Mindfulness and meditation: Using mindfulness and meditation techniques can improve your ability to recognize emotions as they occur and keep you in the present. Techniques for mindfulness let you evaluate your feelings objectively, which lessens impulsive responses.

Deep breathing exercises can relax your nervous system and lessen the physiological effects of strong emotions, such as a quick heartbeat and shallow breathing.

Progressive Muscle Relaxation: Using this method, you gradually tense and then release various muscle groups in your body. It can ease the discomfort brought on by strong emotions.

Grounding Techniques: Exercises that help you focus on your immediate surroundings, such the 5-4-3-2-1 approach, can help you get back on track and relieve mental pain.

Use worksheets or notebooks for emotion control to recognize, categorize, and examine your feelings. You may develop insight and control over your emotional reactions by using this approach.

Emotion-Focused Coping: These coping techniques concentrate on dealing with the emotions themselves rather than the circumstances that brought them on. Self-soothing, self-compassion, and comforting activities are a few examples of techniques.

Cognitive Restructuring: Cognitive-behavioral strategies like cognitive restructuring assist in reframing and challenging erroneous thoughts or a pattern of wrong views that may trigger toxic feeling

Techniques for Distraction: Concentration-demanding activities like hobbies, crossword puzzles, or artistic pursuits can draw your focus away from strong emotions and lessen their influence.

Self-Soothing: Create a toolkit of calming practices for when you're experiencing emotional hardship. This may entail taking a warm bath, drinking herbal tea, or using chamomile or lavender-scented products.

Use of Crisis Plans: Have a crisis plan in place in case your emotions get out of control. This plan should include measures to take in the event that extreme emotions worsen, who to contact for assistance, and what self-help techniques to use.

Time-Outs: When interpersonal confrontations are emotionally charged, think about taking a break to calm down and gather your thoughts. Set a time for the conversation to resume that is convenient for all sides, after they have reached a compromise.

Regular Physical Activity: By encouraging the production of endorphins, which are natural mood enhancers, regular physical activity can help regulate mood and lessen emotional intensity. Keep in mind that emotional control is a talent that takes time to develop. Finding the methods that are most beneficial for you may take some time, and some tactics could be more useful in certain circumstances. You may increase your emotional control and resilience while dealing with BPD if you are persistent and dedicated to improving yourself.

Chapter Seven:
Developing A Self Care Routine

Self-care is not simply a choice while treating Borderline Personality Disorder (BPD); it is a lifeline. This chapter discusses the significance of creating a thorough self-care regimen that is suited to your particular requirements and difficulties. Self-care is a discipline that promotes your physical, emotional, and mental well-being and helps you manage the intricacies of BPD. It goes beyond pampering.

You'll learn as you read this chapter that taking care of yourself is not selfish; rather, it's essential to your long-term stability and mental health. You may better manage the ups and downs of BPD, lessen the effect of symptoms, and enhance your general quality of life by devoting time and effort to creating a self-care regimen that works for you.

7.1 Importance of Self Care

Self-care is essential to controlling Borderline Personality Disorder (BPD) and preserving general mental and emotional health. It is not merely a luxury or a fashionable idea. Self-care is crucial for people with BPD for a number of reasons, many of which cannot be overstated:

Emotional Control: Self-care routines aid in controlling the powerful feelings that BPD sufferers frequently experience. You may avoid feeling overwhelmed emotionally and acting impulsively by engaging in activities that quiet and soothe the mind.

Reducing Stress: Because of the unpredictable nature of emotional changes and interpersonal difficulties, BPD frequently results in increased stress levels. Self-care practices can help you manage your stress and the demands of daily life more effectively.

Self-care increases self-reflection and mindfulness, which leads to an improvement in self-awareness. When your sensitivity can more easily recognize your ideas and feelings.

Improved Coping Skills: Self-care gives you access to a toolbox of coping techniques that you can use when things get tough. You may respond to emotional triggers in a healthier and more positive way by using these abilities.

Building resilience requires regular self-care practices, which help you recover more quickly from difficulties and setbacks. It improves your capacity to withstand any potential emotional turbulence.

Managing BPD may be stressful, and skipping out on self-care can result in burnout. The energy and enthusiasm required to negotiate the complexity of the condition are maintained when you practice regular self-care.

Better Relationships: When you look after your emotional wellbeing, you are better able to form enduring, wholesome bonds with others. Self-care may enhance your relationships with family members and decrease effect of BPD on those relationships.

Self-compassion is an essential part of controlling BPD and is expressed via self-care. You can combat any potential self-criticism and self-doubt by being kind to yourself and putting your wellbeing first.

Overall Quality of Life: In the end, practicing self-care results in an overall improvement in quality of life. It enables you to live more completely and joyfully despite the difficulties associated with BPD.

The significance of self-care cannot be emphasized, but it's critical to understand that there is no one-size-fits-all approach to self-care. You may define self-care differently than others, and it may alter as you mature and develop. This chapter's remaining sections will discuss numerous self-care methods and tactics that you may modify to suit your individual requirements and preferences.

7.2 BPD Self-Care Techniques

A great strategy for overcoming the obstacles posed by Borderline Personality Disorder (BPD) is to establish a self-care regimen suited to your individual requirements. Individuals with BPD may want to think about implementing some of the self-care techniques listed below into their everyday lives:

Exercises in mindfulness and meditation can help you manage strong emotions and remain in the present moment. These techniques can support emotional stability by enabling you to notice your thoughts and feelings without passing judgment.

Deep breathing exercises might help to soothe the nervous system and lessen anxiety. In times of emotional difficulty, deep, diaphragmatic breathing might be very helpful.

Develop a toolkit of tools for regulating emotions, such as naming and classifying emotions, grounding exercises, and self-soothing techniques. These methods assist you in controlling strong emotional responses.

Regular Exercise: Exercise on a regular basis to enhance mood, lower anxiety, and enhance general wellbeing. Find anything you want to do, whether it's yoga, dancing, jogging, or walking.

Healthy Eating: Keep an eye on your nutrition and strive for balanced meals that promote both your physical and mental well-being. Foods high in nutrients can improve mood and energy levels.

A good night's sleep is essential for maintaining mental clarity and emotional equilibrium. Create a calming nighttime ritual and establish a regular sleep regimen.

Journaling: Write your thoughts, feelings, and experiences down in a journal. Writing in a journal gives one a platform for expression and self-examination which give you deeper understanding of your emotional system

Create outlets for your creativity by expressing yourself through the arts, music, writing, or crafts. Using creative avenues to express one's feelings may be beneficial.

Establish a daily schedule that includes regular meals, physical activity, downtime, and sleep. Your day's schedule might help you stay stable and less impulsive.

Social Support: Retain relationships with empathetic friends and family members who can sympathize with your struggles and encourage you.

Therapy: Persevere with dialectical behavior therapy (DBT) or other forms of therapy with a mental health practitioner who specializes in BPD. Therapy can offer direction, skill development, and a secure environment in which to process your feelings.

Reduce Stressors: Recognize and cut back on sources of unneeded stress in your life. This could entail establishing limits,

Self-compassion: Develop self-compassion by being nice and understanding to oneself. Confront self-critical ideas and work on accepting yourself.

Hobbies & Interests: Focus on activities that make you happy and give you a sense of success. Taking part in your favorite hobbies may increase self-confidence and give you a feeling of purpose.

Spend time outside or practice relaxing techniques like taking leisurely walks, having a warm bath, or doing progressive muscle relaxation.

Crisis Plan: Create a crisis plan with the help of your therapist or other mental health specialist. This plan covers emergency contacts and measures to be taken in cases of severe mental distress.

Remember that self-care is an ongoing practice that evolves as your needs change. Experiment with different self-care strategies to discover what works best for you, and be patient with yourself as you develop and maintain your self-care routine. The goal is to build resilience, enhance emotional stability, and improve your overall quality of life while living with BPD.

7.2 Creating a Self-Care Plan

To make self-care a consistent and effective part of your life while managing Borderline Personality Disorder (BPD), it's beneficial to create a structured self-care plan. This plan serves as a roadmap for implementing self-care practices and ensuring that you prioritize your well-being. Here's how to create a personalized self-care plan:

Set precise Goals: Establish clear, precise goals for your own self-care. What results do you want self-care to produce? These objectives may include lessening emotional turbulence, promoting mood stability, or raising general quality of life.

Choose Self-Care Activities: Based on your self-care requirements and objectives, choose the self-care activities you think will be most helpful for you. For ideas, have a look at the list of self-care activities that was previously given.

Set Practice Priorities: Not all self-care techniques should be used simultaneously. Sort them according to their importance for your objectives and present situation. To prevent getting overwhelmed, start with a modest amount of practices.

Establish a Schedule: Create a daily or weekly calendar that includes the self-care techniques of your choice. To reap, consistency is essential self-help.
Set aside particular periods each day for self-care activities that fit with your schedule.

Set Reminders: Use the alarms or reminders on your phone or computer to remind you to practice self-care. When everyday life becomes hectic or stressful, it's simple to forget about or ignore self-care.

Accountability: Tell a family member or friend you can trust about your self-care strategy so they can help hold you responsible. They can provide inspiration and assistance as you strive to keep up your self-care habit.

Flexibility: Be aware that life is dynamic and that there may be days when you are unable to strictly adhere to your self-care plan. Be versatile and flexible, leaving room for changes as needed.

Track Your Progress: Write down the self-care practices you engage in and the effects they have on your wellbeing. Monitoring your progress might help you figure out which techniques are the most successful and inspire you to continue.

Review and Modify: Regularly evaluate your self-care strategy to determine its applicability and efficacy. If your life changes or your requirements for self-care alter, make the necessary adjustments to your plan.

Seek Professional Advice: To make sure your self-care strategy is in line with your therapeutic goals, speak with a therapist or other mental health expert. If required, they can offer advice and make improvements.

Include Crisis techniques: Make sure your self-care plan includes crisis techniques and emergency contacts if you are prone to significant emotional distress or self-harming activities. You must have these for your protection.

Making a self-care plan is a proactive step in putting your wellbeing first and coping with the difficulties brought on by BPD. It offers guidance and structure to help you keep up a regular self-care schedule, ultimately resulting in better overall quality of life and increased emotional stability.

7.3 Getting Past Self-Criticism

Self-criticism is a key obstacle to adequate self-care for people with borderline personality disorder (BPD). The inner critic may be very severe, which can cause feelings of worthlessness and undermine efforts to take care of oneself. Fostering self-compassion and increasing the sustainability of self-care behaviors require overcoming self-criticism:

Start by becoming conscious of your negative beliefs about yourself. When practicing self-care, pay attention to any negative self-talk that could surface. Recognize that self-criticism is not a reflection of your real value but rather a frequent defensive tactic.

Negative ideas should be contested and replaced with ones that emphasize self-compassion. Replace the thought "I don't deserve self-care" with "I am worthy of self-care, and it's necessary for my well-being" whenever you see yourself doing so.

Embrace Self-Compassion: As a fundamental part of your self-care regimen, embrace self-compassion. Be kind, compassionate, and supportive to yourself as you would a good friend going through a similar situation.

Utilize mindfulness methods to impartially notice self-critical thoughts. You may put some distance between these ideas and realize they are only fleeting mental experiences and not actual truths by practicing mindfulness.

Positive affirmations should be a part of your self-care practice. Affirmations such as "I am enough" and "I deserve love and care" should be repeated frequently to help rewire self-critical cognitive patterns.

Seek External Validation: If you have trouble with self-validation, ask dependable family members, friends, or a therapist for support and validation. Self-criticism can have a detrimental effect that can be offset by external validation.

Develop Self-Appreciation: Give yourself some time to reflect on and appreciate your abilities and achievements. Make a list of all of your accomplishments, no matter how tiny, and be proud of them.

Accept Imperfection: Recognize that no one is flawless, and that taking care of oneself is not about being perfect. It's about accepting and nourishing oneself. Accept your flaws as a part of what makes you who you are.

Limit Self-Comparison: Steer clear of comparing oneself to others as this can lead to negative self-talk. Keep in mind that everyone faces obstacles and struggles, even if they are not immediately obvious.

Consider addressing your self-criticism with a therapist or other mental health expert as therapeutic support. Therapy can offer methods and approaches for dealing with self-critical thinking patterns.

The larger objectives of self-care and self-compassion are aligned with the continual process of overcoming self-criticism. You may cultivate a more caring and encouraging mental environment that makes it simpler to prioritize and uphold self-care routines by actively questioning self-critical thoughts and cultivating self-acceptance.

Chapter Eight:
Moving Forward Thriving

In this last chapter, we set out on a mission to thrive despite the obstacles posed by borderline personality disorder (BPD). It is a chapter brimming with inspiration, optimism, and useful advice for embracing a life beyond simply survival.

Although BPD might provide significant challenges, it does not determine who you are or what your future holds. Instead, it provides a backdrop so that your tenacity and fortitude may stand out. This chapter serves as proof that prospering is not only feasible but also very much within your grasp.

We will look at methods for developing a sense of purpose, fostering your hobbies and passions, and defining and accomplishing personal objectives. You'll learn the value of resilience, self-acceptance, and continuous self-improvement. By way of the accounts of

You will have a road plan at the conclusion of this chapter that will help you manage BPD as well as live a life that is joyful, fulfilling, and deeply satisfying. It's a chapter devoted to the amazing journey from just survival to true flourishing.

8.1 Creating Aspirations and Goals

By defining and pursuing important objectives and aspirations, one of the most effective methods to move forward and prosper despite Borderline Personality Disorder (BPD) is possible. Goals provide you focus, direction, and a sense of accomplishment while assisting you in creating a better future. Check out the list of goals setting and achieving techniques.

Establish Your Values: Determine your basic principles and beliefs first. What is most important to you? Knowing your values will help you make more informed decisions, like setting goals that agree with your lifestyle

Set quantifiable Objectives: Be as precise and quantifiable as you can with your objectives. Saying "I want to improve my life" isn't specific enough. Instead, say, "I want to finish a course in a subject I'm passionate about."

Large objectives might feel daunting, so break them down into smaller steps. Divide them up into smaller, more doable actions or goals. This strategy increases the likelihood of success.

Prioritize Your objectives: Decide which of your objectives are most essential to you, then rank them in order of importance. Feeling overwhelmed may be avoided by concentrating on a few main objectives at once.

Establish a realistic timetable for attaining your objectives. A sense of urgency and drive are produced by having a deadline in mind.

Seek Support: Discuss your objectives with a therapist, close friends, or family members who can encourage you and hold you accountable. They can also offer support if necessary.

Honor Your Successes: Honor your successes, no matter how little they may appear. Every step you take toward your objectives is a success that you should celebrate.

Recognize that setbacks are a normal aspect of goal-setting and take them to heart. Consider them as chances for development and learning rather than failures.

Be flexible in your goals and prepared to modify them as necessary if conditions arise. Because life is dynamic, you might need to adjust your goals along the road.

Use visualization techniques to picture yourself succeeding in your endeavors. Visualization can increase confidence and motivation.

Keep Your Commitment: Perseverance and commitment are essential for achieving your goals. Keep in mind the reasons you originally established these goals, even while you are facing difficulties.

Reflect and Revise: Regularly evaluate your progress and make any necessary revisions to your goals. As you mature and change, your ambitions may shift.

Setting and achieving objectives may serve as a potent catalyst for personal development and fulfillment. Your objectives, whether they be for your school, job, relationships, or personal growth, give you a feeling of direction and purpose. You'll discover that you're progressing on your path to thriving with BPD as you strive toward your objectives.

8.3 BPD Self-Care Techniques

Self-care techniques are essential if you want to progress and flourish while treating borderline personality disorder (BPD). You may use these techniques to keep your emotions in check, cultivate self-compassion, and advance your general wellbeing. Here is a closer look at self-care techniques designed for people with BPD:

Establish a daily schedule that incorporates self-care activities. Maintaining a feeling of consistency and predictability in your routine might be very helpful for controlling BPD symptoms.

Emotion Regulation Techniques: Build up your toolbox of emotional control methods, such as progressive muscle relaxation, deep breathing, and mindfulness. You can use these methods to control strong emotions as they occur.

Consider engaging in dialectical behavior therapy (DBT), a treatment strategy created especially for BPD. DBT offers helpful techniques and skills for stress tolerance, interpersonal effectiveness, emotion regulation, and mindfulness.

Develop self-compassion as a crucial component of your self-care practice. Be kind, patient, and understanding to yourself, even when things are tough.

Set and uphold appropriate boundaries in your relationships in order to safeguard your emotional wellbeing. Set clear limits with others and put your own needs first.

Hobbies and interests: Take part in pursuits that make you happy and give you a sense of success. A potent kind of self-care is pursuing your passions.

Journaling: Write in a journal to work through your feelings and thoughts. Keeping a journal might assist you gain understanding of your triggers and behavior patterns.
Social Support: Retain relationships with loved ones and friends who are understanding and encouraging. Share your struggles and experiences with people you can trust.

Put your physical health first by eating a balanced diet, exercising frequently, and getting enough sleep. Emotional balance is intimately related to physical well-being.

Practice relaxation techniques, such as progressive muscle relaxation, deep breathing exercises, or meditation, to lessen tension and anxiety.

Explore your creative side by engaging in activities like writing, music, or painting as a way to express yourself and let out your emotions.

Continue treatment or counseling with a mental health expert who has expertise with BPD for therapeutic support. A safe environment for discovery, skill development, and personal development is provided through therapy.

Practice mindfulness to keep your attention anchored in the here and now. You may see and accept your thoughts and feelings without passing judgment by practicing mindfulness.

Distraction Techniques: When you're feeling down, do something that requires your complete focus, like play a game or work on a puzzle. You can control overpowering emotions through distraction.

Utilize positive affirmations to combat critical self-talk and build self-compassion. Recite affirmations that speak to you to improve your self-esteem.

Crisis Plan: Work with your therapist to create a crisis plan. The procedures to be taken in times of severe emotional distress should be outlined in this plan, along with emergency contacts and self-help techniques.

Keep in mind that there is no one-size-fits-all approach to self-care, and it could take some time to figure out which techniques are most effective for you. Be kind to yourself and make the necessary adjustments to your self-care regimen to fit your changing requirements. In order to thrive while living with BPD, self-care is crucial since it gives you the skills you need to live a happy life.

8.4 Preventing Relapses

Recognizing that relapses or setbacks might happen is essential in the path of flourishing while managing Borderline Personality Disorder (BPD). BPD is characterized by stable intervals interspersed by crisis-filled times. Effective relapse management is crucial to your long-term success. How to handle relapses is as follows:

Recognize Early Warning Signs: Get familiar with the indicators of a possible relapse. Increased emotional ferocity, impulsivity, retreat from social activities, and changes in sleep habits are a few examples of these symptoms.

Seek Professional Assistance: As soon as you become aware of relapse symptoms, get in touch with your therapist or other mental health specialist. If required, they can offer direction, make changes to your treatment plan, or intervene in a crisis.

Engage Your Support Network: During relapses, rely on your network of friends and family for assistance. Talk about your thoughts and experiences with others who can relate to you and be a source of emotional support.

Implement Crisis Plan: Adhere to your crisis plan if you have one. Crisis plans often include instructions on what to do in times of immediate need, such as calling emergency services.

Self-Soothe: To control strong emotions during a relapse, use self-soothing strategies you've learned, such deep breathing, mindfulness, or grounding activities.

Re-examine coping mechanisms and techniques you've learned in therapy, such as dialectical behavior therapy (DBT) techniques. You can use these techniques to help you get through the emotional upheaval of a relapse.

Reduce Overwhelm: To lessen overwhelm during a relapse, divide duties and obligations into smaller, more manageable stages. Prioritize your essential need and self-care until you restore stability.

Avoid Self-Criticism: Self-criticism is a frequent emotion experienced during relapses. Practice self-compassion and remind yourself that setbacks are a normal part of rehabilitation rather than berating yourself.

Relapses are chances for learning and progress, so take use of them. Examine the factors that led to the relapse and consider how to avoid or better handle similar circumstances in the future.

Management of medicine: If you are taking medicine, be sure you are doing it according to the directions. Any worries or adverse effects should be brought up with the prescribed healthcare professional.

Maintain Contact: Even when you're not experiencing a crisis, maintain contact with your therapist or other mental health expert. Regular check-ins can offer continuous assistance and help prevent relapses.

Identify and eliminate causes of unneeded stress in your life to lessen stress. Stress can make BPD symptoms worse and raise the possibility of recurrence.

Crisis Helplines: Become familiar with the hotlines or crisis helplines you can call in an emergency. having access to assistance from professionals

Relapse management is not a sign of failure; rather, it is an inevitable part of the journey. You may lessen the effects of relapses and continue on your journey to flourishing with BPD by recognising them and taking proactive steps to treat them. Your perseverance in the face of obstacles is evidence of your tenacity and resolve.

8.5 Resources and Assistance

It might be difficult to navigate Borderline Personality Disorder (BPD), but you don't have to do it alone. You have access to a wide range of tools and support systems that can help you on your path to success. How to access these priceless materials is as follows:

Continue your treatment or counseling sessions; preferably, this should be done with a mental health practitioner who has expertise with BPD or dialectical behavior therapy (DBT). Therapy offers a disciplined and a favorable environment for development.

Support Groups: Sign up for an online forum or group for people with BPD. These groups offer a secure setting where members may open up about their experiences, learn from those who have overcome similar obstacles, and give and receive support and encouragement. Crisis Helplines: Become familiar with the 24-hour crisis helplines or hotlines. When someone is experiencing severe emotional distress, these crisis hotlines offer instant assistance.

Explore online resources and mental health applications that include coping mechanisms, self-help tools, and mood monitoring. These applications can help you further and contribute to your self-care regimen.

Books and Publications: There are a lot of books and publications that have been published by professionals and people who have lived with BPD. Reading these items can offer insightful information, coping mechanisms, and a feeling of community.

Participate in educational seminars or workshops on BPD and related subjects. These gatherings can increase your knowledge and provide you chances to interact with professionals and peers.

Connect with advocacy groups that are concerned with BPD and mental health. These groups frequently provide access to resources, information, and chances to get involved in advocacy and awareness initiatives.

Medication Management: Keep in regular contact with your prescribing healthcare professional if medication is a component of your treatment plan. Discuss any worries or side effects, and carefully adhere to all drug directions.

Peer Support: Speak with those who have successfully controlled BPD for peer support. Their life lessons and perspectives might provide you inspiration and useful advice for your own journey. Neighborhood Resources Investigate community services and resources for mental health in your area that provide assistance, guidance, and educational materials related to BPD.

Engage your family and friends as part of your support system. Share your own stories with them, enlighten them about BPD, and let them know how they may be of greatest assistance.

Use credible internet sources, websites, and discussion groups that are dedicated to BPD and mental health. These platforms have the potential to offer helpful information and a feeling of community.

Keep in mind that asking for assistance and encouragement indicates strength, not weakness. There are people and resources available to help you along the way, so you are not traveling alone. You may empower yourself to thrive despite the obstacles of BPD by creating a network of support and gaining access to helpful resources.

8.6 Future Prospects

It's crucial to maintain the steadfast conviction that there is hope for a better future despite the complexity of Borderline Personality Disorder (BPD). Your guiding light can be hope, which can show you the way to a life of contentment, development, and resiliency. How to grow and preserve optimism for the future is as follows:

appreciate Your Progress: Regardless of how little it may be, acknowledge and appreciate your progress. Each stride you take ahead is evidence of your tenacity and will.
Set Achievable Goals: Choose goals that are both inspiring and attainable. These objectives act as lighthouses of hope that inspire you to work for a brighter future.

Embrace good Influences: Surround yourself with good influences, whether they come in the form of encouraging companions, admirable role models, or upbeat reading material. Positivity might energize your hope and improve your spirits.
Think about the future you want to build while you spend time imagining it. Through visualization, you may increase your sense of achievability and strengthen your resolve.

Maintain Your Commitment to Self-Care: Continue to practice self-care activities that support emotional stability and wellbeing. By reassuring you of your capacity to care for yourself, self-care fosters optimism.

Draw strength from your network of friends, family, therapists, and support groups by leaning on them. Their support and compassion might help you maintain hope when things are difficult.

Learn from Obstacles: See obstacles and failures as chances for development and education. They are not obstacles in your path to a better future; rather, they are detours.

Develop Resilience: Put your energy on enhancing your capacity for overcoming hardship. Your optimism and belief in your capacity to get beyond problems are strengthened by resilience.

Accept Change: Be receptive to alteration and personal development. A more optimistic view and unexpected chances might result from accepting change.

Engage in mindfulness exercises to stay in the present and develop a sense of serenity and acceptance. You may better appreciate each moment's potential and beauty by practicing mindfulness.

Consider telling people about your experiences and journey, whether through writing, speaking, or advocacy. Others struggling with comparable problems may find hope in your tale.

Continue to seek advice from mental health specialists who are knowledgeable with BPD. They can offer assistance and solutions that are specifically designed to help you develop hope for the future.

Keep in mind that hope is a dynamic force that propels good change; it is not a passive feeling. It is the conviction that better days are attainable and that you are getting closer to the future you desire with each step you take. Your path is a monument to your fortitude, and while you advance and flourish with BPD, hope is your continuous companion.

Conclusion

I want to underline as we get to the end of this book, "Borderline Personality Disorder Survival Guide," that your experience with BPD is defined by your remarkable resilience, strength, and ability for growth rather than by the difficulties you have faced. You have persevered through the darkest nights, navigated through the heights of emotional turmoil, and confronted times of despondency. You have come out of it all a survivor, a warrior, and someone who has a great deal of potential for a better future.

We have looked at the complexities of BPD in these pages, including its symptoms, diagnosis, effects on relationships, self-worth, and daily living. Effective coping mechanisms, the value of self-care, and the influence of self-compassion have all been taught to you. You've explored the realm of emotions and learned techniques for controlling strong emotions and preserving emotional stability. You've learned more about establishing objectives, growing hope, and prospering in the face of difficulties.

To be clear, though, your trip is just getting started; this is not its conclusion. You have the ability to design a life that is meaningful, joyful, and fulfilling. The knowledge you've gained and the abilities you've honed are your resources for creating a future that goes beyond BPD's limitations.

Your Travels Are Special: Keep in mind that your experience with BPD is entirely personal. Although you could have similar experiences to those of other BPD sufferers, your road to recovery and success is unique. Honor your accomplishments and embrace your uniqueness. Your resilience and your capacity for improvement define you, not your diagnosis or your history.

The necessity of asking for assistance and creating a support system has been underlined throughout this book. Keep in mind that asking for help is a tremendous indication of strength, not weakness. There are people and resources available to aid you along this journey, so you are not traveling alone.

Setting realistic expectations for yourself is essential as you go forward on your journey. There are ups and downs throughout the recovery process; it is not a straight line. There will be successful and challenging times. But in such trying times, you have a chance to exhibit extraordinary resiliency and perseverance.

Hold onto hope with unyielding persistence. Hope is Your Guiding Light. Having hope is a dynamic, active feeling a power that helps you advance. It is the conviction that brighter days are not only conceivable but indeed unavoidable. Your experience is proof of the eternal power of hope.

Adopt Self-Compassion: Adopt self-compassion above all else. As you would a close friend, treat yourself with care, patience, and understanding. Replace your judgment and self-criticism with love and compassion. All the love and compassion in the world are yours for the taking.

Let's end by praising your bravery, resiliency, and dedication to thriving despite BPD's difficulties. Your journey involves transformation and progress rather than merely ensuring your existence. It is a journey that reveals the limitless potential you possess.

Keep in mind that each step you take after finishing these pages is evidence of your perseverance and your ability to live a life that is purposeful, joyful, and fulfilling. Your fortitude and resiliency, not your diagnoses, are what make you who you are. You have limitless opportunities ahead of you, and I have no doubt that you'll seize them with enthusiasm.

I wish you a future filled with healing, growth, and thriving with hope as your compass, self-compassion as your continuous companion, and the understanding that you are never alone on this journey. May your life serve as an example of the remarkable fortitude of the human spirit.

As you continue on your adventure, the best is yet to come.

Once more thank you for patronizing us. If you got value from this masterpiece, kindly go back to Amazon and drop a review, it will help us to do more.